IMAGES
of America

DORCHESTER

IMAGES
of America

DORCHESTER

Anthony Mitchell Sammarco

ARCADIA

First printed in 1995.
Reprinted in 2000, 2001.

Published by Arcadia Publishing,
an imprint of Tempus Publishing, Inc.
2A Cumberland Street
Charleston, SC 29401

Printed in Great Britain.

For all general information contact Arcadia Publishing at:
Telephone 843-853-2070
Fax 843-853-0044
E-Mail sales@arcadiapublishing.com

For customer service and orders:
Toll-Free 1-888-313-2665

Visit us on the internet at http://www.arcadiapublishing.com

Contents

From Farming Town
to City Annex

Dorchester was formally annexed to Boston on January 4, 1870, marking the death of an independent town originally founded in 1630 by a band of Puritans seeking religious freedom.

The town of Dorchester, which was composed primarily of farms and industrial firms along the Neponset River, was wealthy and well-placed. The shore, fronting on Dorchester Bay and near woodlands to the west, supplied early settlers with food and building materials. The water power afforded by the Neponset River enabled settlers to fund the first grist mill in the United States and the various other industries which sustained the settlement.

By 1830, Dorchester was an agreeable town of about 2,000 residents, most of whom were farmers. The development was minimal, and much of the land was still owned by descendants of early settlers.

Dorchester Turnpike, now Dorchester Avenue, was cut through the town in 1804, and connected Boston to the Lower Mills. The new road, well over 9 miles in length, created an even-paced and fairly straight route to the industries at Neponset.

The idea of separation of church and state began to be debated in the early nineteenth century. The First Parish Church on Meeting House Hill had been the only "meetinghouse" in Dorchester from 1630 until 1806, when a small group of the congregation chose to establish another church. The reasons were varied, but one factor was the increase in population which resulted in overcrowding in the old church.

Also, divergence in religious beliefs was spreading across the country. The First Parish Church had adopted Unitarianism, a belief that rejects the doctrine of the Trinity and asserts the oneness of God and the teachings of Christ. The group that formed the new parish in the town were considered orthodox Congregationalists, who aspired to the independence of each local church. This could be construed as a direct descent from the Puritan ideology of 1630. The break in 1806, though amicable, was to propel the town into a religious separation that would last for decades.

The divergence culminated in the establishment of the Town Hall in 1816. The Town Hall was to be the meeting place for all political and town business in Dorchester until 1870. Located in Baker's Corners (Codman Square), the site was in the geographical center of Dorchester.

The hall was a brick building, with a Greek portico, which might have echoed the democratic ideals emanating from Greece in the early nineteenth century. With the establishment of the Town Hall, the separation of the two churches was complete. No longer were either the First Parish Church or the Old South (later to be known as the Second Church) in competition to "host" town meetings.

The town's rural bounty is evident in two handsome landscapes in the collection of the Dorchester Historical Society. *Savin Hill*, painted by Michael O. Barry in 1830, shows the area with only two houses; *Commercial Point* shows the area of the Boston Gas tanks, at that time an industrial community that combined both mills and residences.

Point Industry, obliterated in 1882, was a thriving area with docks that allowed both clipper ships and whaling vessels to dock in Dorchester. The whaling business lasted only about a decade, from 1835 to 1845, but the port continued to thrive. The area known as Glover's Corners, where Freeport Street and Dorchester Avenue intersect, was irreverently known as "Sodom and Gomorrah" since the town landing seemed to attract the sailors and women from the port area to the taverns and inns located on the eastern slope of Meeting House Hill.

By 1840, with the Old Colony Railroad under construction in Dorchester, the first aspects of development were occurring. Harrison Square was laid out by Luther Briggs Jr., a local architect who not only created a street-grid pattern, but built substantial Italianate houses throughout the area.

The area today is fondly known as Clam Point, but it was officially named in 1841 in memory of President William Henry Harrison, who died in office. He had campaigned in Dorchester and public grief over his untimely death led to the commemorative naming of the square. The residential area was later transformed into commercial development, as the Putnam Nail Company, the Pope Lumber Company, and A.T. Stearns' Lumber Company commenced business.

From 1850 to 1870, commerce expanded and residential development also increased. Housing was needed for all the workers and managers. Without them, the factories could not operate. The housing boom had arrived, and, by the time of the Civil War, Dorchester's population had swollen to about 10,000 residents. The possibility of annexation began to seem more real. But the annexation movement had both supporters and detractors, each believing their way would most benefit the town.

The supporters were mostly well-to-do merchants who had moved to Dorchester because the Old Colony Railroad made access to Boston convenient, and they strongly advocated that the town must accept the inevitable. The detractors were mostly farmers and old family members from the pre-Revolution days, and they held out for the maintenance of the town as an independent entity. The two sides held raucous meetings at Town Hall, and numerous broadsides were published both supporting and denouncing the proposed annexation.

By the end of the Civil War, in 1865, the town was divided. The supporters of annexation, led by Marshall P. Wilder of Washington Street, were adamant. The old Dorchester families who opposed annexation owned most of the land, so their votes would carry much weight.

But annexation was voted in, with 928 votes in favor and 726 opposed. The 202 votes that allowed the annexation had ensured that all future "town meetings" would take the form of "ward meetings" as Dorchester became a ward of the City of Boston.

The last Dorchester Town Meeting was held in the Town Hall on December 28, 1869. The last reports of the selectmen—descendants of the first form of town government in the United States, founded in 1633—were accepted, and votes of thanks were proffered to the selectmen for their work on behalf of the town.

With annexation a reality, the concept of town life changed. The City of Boston took possession of all aspects of town life in Dorchester on January 4, 1870. The results were immense, with property values increasing ten-fold as real estate prices inflated almost overnight. Developers had begun to change the town with new buildings and streets, but the Panic of 1876 caused a stoppage in the uncontrolled development. In the years prior to 1880, Dorchester had seen tremendous growth and change.

The "Forty Years to Annexation" composed four decades of strange and new adventures for a town already 240 years old. The name "Dorchester" will never die, although our ancestors' decision to opt for urban living changed the rural town of their lifetime into the urban streetscape of ours.

One

Savin Hill and Glover's Corner

The Tuttle House was at the corner of Savin Hill Avenue and Tuttle Street. One of Boston's first seaside hotels, it was owned by Joseph Tuttle, who renamed "Old Hill" as "Savin Hill" in 1822. Savin trees covered the hill that projected into Dorchester Bay.

Barracks were built on Savin Hill at the time of the Revolutionary War. Grampian Way has a panoramic view of Boston and the Harbor, and these small buildings were built on the north side of the Way.

"Mayfield" was the home of John J. May, a Boston merchant, who built his house on Dorchester Avenue at the corner of Mayfield Street. May was the first president of the Dorchester Historical Society, which was founded in 1891.

The Hoag House at 210 Savin Hill Avenue is typical of the houses that were built in Dorchester following annexation. This large, mansard-roofed house was built by the Darling family, and for the last century has been the home of the Hoag family.

Savin Hill, seen here from Commercial Point, was a steep hill of rocks covered with Savin trees. As late as the 1840s, only two houses were on Savin Hill proper. However, with the coming of the Old Colony Railroad, commuters began to settle in the area because of the accessibility to Boston.

This view from Grampian Way on Savin Hill, towards Boston and Dorchester Bay, is breathtaking. On the far left is the neighborhood of Savin Hill, which extends to Columbia Road. The Old Colony Railroad tracks were replaced with the MBTA and the open land was developed for *The Boston Globe* in the 1950s. South Boston and Telegraph Hill (Dorchester Heights) can be seen in the distance, on the right.

The Bowman House was on Pleasant Street, near Glover's Corner. Built by Reverend Jonathan Bowman, it was the home of the town minister from 1729 until his death in 1775.

"Rosebank" was the house of Alexander Hamilton Wood, a Boston merchant who built his house on Savin Hill Avenue. A Victorian extravaganza, it boasted turrets, gables, and wings, with a carriage house in the rear. The house was demolished when the Southeast Expressway was developed, and the area excavated for development.

The Carriage House of the Wood Estate had twelve horse stalls, with living-space above for the coachmen and grooms. The well-kept lawns and flower beds were an attraction. The family dog posed for this photograph.

Regattas were held in Dorchester Bay during the summer months. On the right is the Savin Hill Yacht Club, still located on the Bay.

This photograph of the Savin Hill Yacht Club and the launches in the foreground show how many members of the yacht club kept boats at Savin Hill. Morrissey Boulevard is now located on the left.

With such close proximity to the ocean, Dorchester has always had a marine connection. Here, workers at Savin Hill repair and paint small boats and yachts in dry dock.

Glover's Corner is the junction of Dorchester Avenue and Freeport, Hancock, and East Streets. In the eighteenth century it was the town landing, and ships docked here. With such a large number of sailors, who had been at sea for many months, there proliferated taverns, inns, and "painted ladies" at the Corner, and it gained the appellation "Sodom and Gomorrah."

The Farrington Store was at the corner of Dorchester Avenue and East Street. A large building with a rough, stone first floor, it was where one could obtain groceries, brooms, and pails, as well as tools. The store was originally opened by the Glover family, and the Corner is named for them.

Hancock Street, just west of Glover's Corner and around the corner from the Farrington Store, had small, workers' houses, as well as more stores.

The Old Dorchester Clubhouse was a large club composed of members who were born in Dorchester. Built at the corner of Pleasant and Pearl Streets, it is now a meeting hall of the Knights of Columbus.

Theodore White, a noted historian and author, was born and raised on Erie Street in Grove Hall. Dorchester had one of the largest population of Jews in New England in the early twentieth century.

Two
Grove Hall

Grove Hall, at the junction of Warren Street and Blue Hill Avenue, marked the boundary between Roxbury (left) and Dorchester. Grove Hall was named after the estate of T.K. Jones in the early nineteenth century, and by 1900 it had become a thriving commercial center.

"Hawthorne Grove" was the estate of Marshall Pinckney Wilder. Originally built by Governor Increase Sumner, it was greatly enlarged when Wilder laid out greenhouses and orchards. Wilder was a hybridizer, and his camellias were among the finest to be developed in the nineteenth century.

Marshall Pinckney Wilder's estate was at the corner of Washington Street and Columbia Road. A Boston merchant, he served as president of the Massachusetts Horticultural Society, and was instrumental in founding both the State Agricultural College and the United States Agricultural Society.

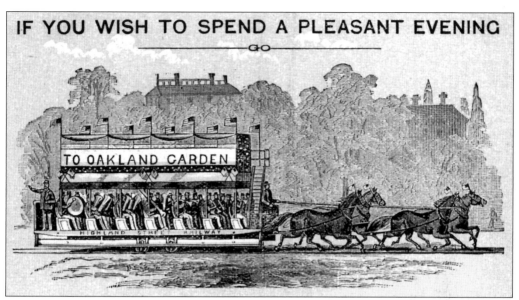

IF YOU WISH TO SPEND A PLEASANT EVENING

GO

TO OAKLAND GARDEN

So popular were the attractions of Oakland Garden that horse-drawn omnibuses were chartered from the Highland Railway. Thus, "if you wish to spend a pleasant evening," all you had to do was purchase a ticket! The large numbers of visitors not only took the omnibuses but walked from miles around.

Oakland Garden was an outdoor amusement park, located on Columbia Road near Blue Hill Avenue. Evening performances included mini-theatricals, operettas, and concerts, while circuses and sideshows amused local children during the day.

OAKLAND GARDEN
GROVE HALL

TAKE
HIGHLAND RAILWAY CARS,

21

The Wales House was on Columbia Road, just east of Oldfields Street. This house, with its substantial amount of land, was later developed with numerous houses in the early twentieth century. Notice the orchard to the left.

The Grove Hall Universalist Church was built in 1894 at the corner of Washington and Wilder Streets. Designed by Francis R. Allen, it still commands attention as one passes through Grove Hall.

Seen from Mount Bowdoin, Washington Street (in the foreground) had been developed with three-deckers by the turn of the century. In the background, the New York, New Haven, and Hartford train passes through "Red Top" village, a development laid out in the 1880s with houses that sported red roof tiles.

The Gleason Street Congregational Church was built as a small, shingle-style church in the newly laid-out area of Harvard Street. It later merged with the Second Church in Dorchester.

The Ripley House (right) was at the corner of Harvard and Bicknell Streets, and it was here that the Dorchester Women's Club was founded. The Bicknell House (left) was built in the early nineteenth century when the area was mostly farmland.

Clara Smith Ripley and her husband, Charles Ripley, built their Dorchester house in 1879. They were thought a "progressive family," as one neighbor recalled, and their house was later to become the "Grey House" of Saint Leo's Church.

Three
Edward Everett Square

Five Corners, in the mid-nineteenth century, had a bucolic quality. The Edward Everett House (left) was built in 1746 by the Oliver family, and is now the site of a Dunkin Donuts. The Davenport House (right) is now the site of a Kentucky Fried Chicken.

The James Blake House, Boston's oldest house, originally stood on Massachusetts Avenue just north of Everett Square. In 1895, it was relocated to Richardson Park for the purpose of preservation, and restored by the architect Charles Hodgdon as an example of seventeenth-century architecture. This photograph shows the Blake House prior to its moving.

The Captain Lemuel Clap House was enlarged in 1765, from an earlier house built c. 1710. It was known as "Willow Court," because, in the nineteenth century, there were five willow trees, with a combined girth of 105 inches, leading to the house. Though originally located about 500 feet from the street, the house was moved to its present location, at the corner of Boston and Enterprise Streets, in 1957.

The William Clapp House was built in 1806 and referred to as the "Mansionhouse" by the Clapp family. A substantial Federal house, it had an ell added for servants in 1839. Today it is the headquarters of the Dorchester Historical Society, founded in 1891 to preserve, collect, and publish the history of Dorchester.

William Clapp was a town selectman and representative to the Great and General Court. A tanner by trade, he later established orchards where he and his sons Lemuel, Thaddeus, and Frederick Clapp hybridized various fruits. One successful pear hybridization was "Clapp's Favorite," a cross between Flemish Beauty and Bartlett pears.

The Andrews Estate was at the corner of Columbia Road and Dorchester Avenue, and was a magnificent Italianate mansion surrounded by gardens. Notice the orchards to the left of the carriage entrance.

The Fox House was at the corner of Mayhew and Boston Streets. Built in 1845, this Greek Revival house survived until 1913, when it was demolished for the new Saint Margaret's Convent.

This photograph was taken looking east from the bridge of the New York, New Haven, and Hartford Railroad, on West Cottage Street. This street had been laid out and developed with small houses by the time of the Civil War.

The Simpson House on West Cottage Street was a substantial, mansard-roofed duplex, built for new residents moving to Dorchester in the 1860s, an era of fervid speculation in the property market. Set on small lots of land, these new houses were built for the aspiring middle class.

Originally known as "Five Corners," the junction of Columbia Road and Boston, East Cottage, and West Cottage Streets was renamed "Edward Everett Square" in memory of one of Dorchester's finest sons. The traffic circle in the foreground was the site of Everett's statue until the 1930s, when one-too-many traffic accidents forced the statue to be moved for safety to Richardson Park.

Saint Margaret's Church was built at the corner of Columbia Road and Dorchester Avenue. Designed by Keeley and Houghton and built in 1894, this impressive Romanesque church was designed for the rapidly-growing Roman Catholic population in Dorchester.

Four
Meeting House Hill

Meeting House Hill has been the site of the First Parish Church as well as the Mather School (left), the first school in America to be supported by taxation. The school was founded in 1639 and the present Mather School, designed by Cram, Goodhue, and Ferguson, is Dorchester's pride and joy. The Lyceum Hall is on the right.

The First Parish Church was originally built at "Five Corners," but in 1670 it was moved a mile south, by oxen, to the hill that has been known henceforth as Meeting House Hill. This photograph shows the fifth meeting house, built in 1816 and destroyed by fire in 1896.

The old Mather School (right) was dwarfed by the new schoolhouse built in 1905. The progress of public education in Boston has been tremendous.

ADMIT THE BEARER

TO THE

DEDICATION OF LYCEUM HALL,

Thursday Evening, February 27, '40,

TO COMMENCE AT HALF PAST 6 O'CLOCK.

JOHN H. ROBINSON, SEC'Y.

Lyceum Hall was an impressive Greek Revival building, designed as a place for lectures, exhibitions, dances, and other town events that included the induction of local soldiers entering the Civil War. By 1891, it became a special needs school of the city of Boston, and was demolished in 1955.

Eaton Tavern was kept by Percival Eaton, and later by his son Ebenezer Eaton, at Eaton Square, directly opposite Saint Peter's Church, from the time of the Revolution until the Civil War.

INDEPENDENCE.

Admit Mr.

To Capt. EATON's Hall, in Dorchester, on TUESDAY, JULY 4th, 1809. at 2 o'clock, P. M.

E. M. SMITH, } Chairman Com. Arrangements.

A ticket to an Independence Day party at Eaton Hall, held on July 4, 1809, shows that not only were dances held here, but the Union Lodge of Masons met here for many years. A local wag, Ebenezer Eaton, upon being rebuked for his profanity by a deacon of the First Parish Church, once said "Deacon, my swearing is like your praying. Neither one of us means anything by it!"

34

Meeting House Hill, seen here from Mount Bowdoin, was an impressive site overlooking Dorchester Bay. In the foreground is Saint Mary's Church, with the First Parish Church directly behind. This rural view of Dorchester shows a town that was to be annexed to Boston less than three decades later.

Saint Mary's Church was Dorchester's first Episcopal church, built at the corner of Bowdoin and Topliff Streets. The nave of the church shows a simple country church, although the building was designed by a noted Boston architect, Arthur Gilman, in 1861.

The Harris-Capen House, or "Mount Ida" as it was known, was built in 1793 at the summit of Bird's Hill, just west of Meeting House Hill. Sold by Reverend Harris in 1840, it became the home of the Nahum Capen family until 1916, when it was demolished and the estate became Ronan Park.

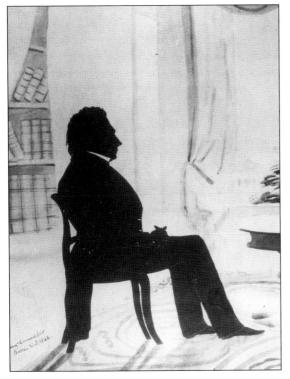

Reverend Thaddeus Mason Harris was the minister of the First Parish Church of Dorchester from 1793 to 1840. His silhouette was cut by August Edouart, in Harris' library at "Mount Ida."

36

The Front Hall of "Mount Ida" was redecorated by the Capens in 1840, with the addition of scenic wallpaper and ingrained carpeting. The house remained virtually unchanged until the death of Edward Nahum Capen in 1916.

Cracker Hollow was the area that is now the intersection of Bowdoin Street and Geneva Avenue. The Samuel Davenport House (right) and Friendship Hall, where dances were often held, were side by side.

The First Parish Church was founded in 1630 and located upon the hill that, by 1670, would bear its name. This photograph, taken *c.* 1870, provides an image of a country town's common, with the meetinghouse rising from the hill.

The vestry of the First Parish Church was designed by Edwin J. Lewis Jr., a noted local architect. Seen from the doorway, below a Colonial Revival musicians' gallery, is the Allen Parlor, named for Thomas Allen, a Boston merchant and member of the church, whose portrait can be seen above the mantle. The Allen Parlor was later dedicated also to the memory of Reverend James K. Allen, minister from 1954 until 1991.

Adams Street, here looking north towards Meeting House Hill, remained relatively rural in the 1870s, with the Fox-May House (left) and the Hall House (right).

"Underhill" was the home of the May family and is at the corner of Adams and Fox Streets. Built by John Fox in the 1850s, and probably designed by Luther Briggs Jr., the house still stands at 69 Adams Street, though hemmed in by three-deckers on all sides.

Meeting House Hill is depicted in this scene in 1847, with the First Parish Church opposite the town common, and Lyceum Hall on the right. Founded in Plymouth, England, in 1630, before the Puritans sailed on the *Mary and John*, this church is the oldest religious society in Boston. Seen in this print are Ebenezer Eaton's three cows, Mr. Williams (the local schoolteacher), and

"Uncle" Daniel Davenport (the sexton and town gravedigger, shown with his wheelbarrow). The trees are protected by wood sheaths that prevented horses and cows from chewing the bark from the young trees.

Known today as "The Manse," this building was built by the Swan family on High Street in the 1830s, and has been the parsonage of the First Parish Church for nearly sixty years.

Mrs. Saunders' and Miss Beach's Academy was built in 1804, at the corner of Adams and East Streets. Here, a young lady would be taught embroidery, sewing, geography, how to play the pianoforte, and a smattering of French . . . everything she would need to know as an adult!

The Almshouse, or the "Dorchester Poor House," was at Kane Square, the junction of Bowdoin and Hancock Streets. Built at the town's expense, it was a place where the "worthy needy" might find relief from creditors and cares.

The Soldiers Monument was erected in 1867 by the Pickwick Club, a society of men who had attended Dorchester High School. The obelisk, on a granite plinth base, commemorated the soldiers from Dorchester who had died during the Civil War.

Saint Peter's Church was built in 1872 from the stone upon which it rises. Patrick Keeley, the foremost Catholic architect in America, quarried the puddingstone ledges at the corner of Bowdoin and Percival Streets, and built a magnificent and impressive church that, ironically, shared a named with St. Peter's, the Anglican church in Dorchester, Dorset, England, from which the Puritans had come in 1630.

Reverend Peter Ronan was the first curate of Saint Peter's Church on Meeting House Hill. Immensely popular, he had the noted architect Patrick Keeley design a "puddingstone" church that would rival any urban church. Ronan Park was named for him in 1909.

The nave of Saint Peter's Church has impressive roof trusses, with elaborate, hand-carved woodwork. The seating capacity of the church is well over one thousand people, and it quickly became a stronghold of Catholic belief in Dorchester.

The convent of Saint Peter's Church (right) was built at the corner of Bowdoin Street and Mount Ida Road, the former carriage drive to the Harris-Capen House. The rectory and Saint Peter's Church made for an impressive streetscape on Meeting House Hill.

Patrick Collins, a noted attorney and onetime mayor of Boston, built his home on Percival Street, overlooking Dorchester Bay. This Italianate house had extensive grounds that were subdivided, in the early years of the twentieth century, into three-deckers.

Patrick Collins was mayor of Boston when he died in 1905. As an attorney and statesman, he proved that someone who was born in Ireland had as much of a chance of making his mark as anyone else in Boston.

Five
Upham's Corner

Upham's Corner was the junction of Boston (now Columbia Road), Dudley, and Stoughton Streets. The general store, kept by Amos Upham, was a Federal house that was converted to commercial purposes in 1802.

The Swan House was designed by Charles Bulfinch as a summerhouse for James and Hepzibah Clarke Swan. Built at the corner of Dudley and Howard Streets, it was an impressive house with a decidedly French feeling. Mrs. Swan received the Marquise de Lafayette here in 1824, when he made his triumphant tour in celebration of the 50th anniversary of the American Revolution.

The Humphreys House had stood at the corner of Dudley and Humphreys Streets since 1634, with additions being made over the next two centuries. By 1918, the house was a virtual museum of Humphrey family memorabilia. The encroachment of commercialism, in the early twentieth century, forced the Humphreys to move to Brookline, but not before the interior of the Humphreys House was photographed. Ironically, portions of the house were re-used in a new house on Fayerweather Street in Cambridge, Massachusetts.

The Morton-Taylor House was designed by Charles Bulfinch for his cousin Sarah Wentworth Apthorp Morton and her husband, Perez Morton. A noted writer, Mrs. Morton wrote *A Power of Sympathy* here, which is considered America's first novel. The house, a distinguished Georgian mansion, stood at the corner of Dudley and Burgess Streets.

The Carriage House and the greenhouses of the Morton-Taylor House ran along Dudley Street.

The "Steamboat House," so named as it was thought to resemble one, was at the corner of Pleasant Street and Sawyer Avenue. Built in 1804, the house later had additions made for new rooms. By the 1880s, brick row houses had been built on Pleasant Street facing the house, and in 1916 the "Steamboat House" was demolished and three-deckers built on its site.

The Stoughton Tomb at the Old North Burying Ground was erected after the death of Governor William Stoughton in 1701. He bequeathed his estate to Harvard College, where Stoughton Hall was erected and perpetuates his name.

The Old North Burying Ground was laid out in 1634 as a "five rod square enclosure." The Puritans who settled Dorchester are buried here, as well as Governors Stoughton and Tailor, General Humphrey Atherton of the Ancient and Honorable Artillery Company, and generations of families.

"Uncle" Daniel Davenport was the sexton of the First Parish Church and the gravedigger at the Old North Burying Ground. He dug fellow-townsmens' graves for forty-nine years, and even prepared his own years before it was needed. He was succeeded by his son, William Davenport.

"Oakland" was the home of Robert Chamblet Hooper, a Boston merchant, who had Luther Briggs Jr. design his house on a hill just west of Upham's Corner. The estate was large, and was later subdivided, with Lingard, Hooper, Chamblet, Half Moon, and Robin Hood Streets being laid out through the former estate.

The Everett-Appleton House was on Pleasant Street, the present site of the Edward Everett School. Built in 1779 by Moses Everett, minister of the First Parish Church and uncle of Edward Everett, the house was demolished in 1909, when the school was built.

The Gardner-Trull House was on Hancock Street, opposite Trull Street. A substantial Greek Revival mansion, it was the home of Governor Gardner and, later, John Trull, a land developer and speculator. Trull owned much of the land west of his house, and laid it out as Howe, Rill, Trull, and Glendale Streets.

The Dyer House stood on Columbia Road, beside the Baker Memorial Church. Built by the Clapp family in 1810, it was later purchased by Micah Dyer, a Boston attorney, who made extensive changes to the exterior. It was demolished in 1918 to make way for the Strand Theatre.

Built by local architect John A. Fox, 44 Virginia Street is the epitome of a stick-style house in Dorchester. With a projecting porch and a fanciful porch roof, its use of stick style and shingle detailing made for an impressive house. Most recently, this house was the rectory to Saint Kevin's Church on Columbia Road.

John A. Fox was a distinguished architect who designed numerous stick-style houses in Dorchester, and, later, firehouses, commercial structures, hospitals, and insane asylums. Seen here in his Boston architectural office at 120 Tremont Street, he began his career as a surveyor, and later studied architecture with Ware and Van Brundt before practicing on his own.

Seen here from Payson Avenue, Jones Hill was being developed with large houses in the late nineteenth century. Hancock Street (in the foreground) is being "rolled" following the Great Blizzard of 1888. The former Dexter Greene House (upper left) had been converted into Saint Mary's Infant Asylum, later Saint Margaret's Hospital.

The headquarters of the American Temperance Society were located at 23 Trull Street, in a house designed by John A. Fox and built beside his own house (left). These substantial houses on small lots of land began to spring up, as if by magic, after Dorchester was annexed to Boston in 1870.

Mary Hunt was the president of the American Temperance Society, a nationwide organization that expounded on the idea that living without alcohol was clean living! Moving from Hyde Park, a section of Dorchester that incorporated itself as a separate town in 1868, she came to Dorchester in 1893, and continued her quest for an alcohol-free society.

The John C. Clapp House was designed by the owner, and built at the corner of Salcomb and Peverell Streets. Clapp was descended from the family that had settled in Dorchester in 1633, and Salcomb Street was named to commemorate Salcombe Regis, the town from which the Clapps had emigrated to Dorchester.

This spectacular view is from the John C. Clapp House looking toward Dorchester Bay. The houses in the foreground are on Peverell Street.

The Trotter House still stands at 97 Sawyer Avenue, and has been declared a landmark on the National Register of Historic Places. Here a student from the Edward Everett School reads the marker to his fellow students.

William Monroe Trotter was a Harvard-educated publisher. His newspaper, *The Guardian*, was an important voice of the African-American community. The son of James Monroe Trotter, a teacher and employee of the United States Post Office, William Monroe Trotter would help to found the Niagra Movement, the predecessor of the NAACP.

Cushing Avenue, looking towards Columbia Road, shows the extent of the development of Upham's Corner at the turn of the century. On the left is the roof turret of 15 Cushing Avenue, and the Baker Memorial Church is on the corner. On the right are two family houses on Cushing Avenue, which backed up to commercial structures along Stoughton Street.

"Hillside" was the estate of the Thacher family, built on terracing facing Stoughton Street. Windemere Road was once the carriage drive to the house, which became the Harley Hospital after the family moved to Percival Street. Today, a tar-topped parking lot marks the site of this elegant mansion.

The Federal general store of Amos Upham was replaced in 1884 by a one-story, brick and granite structure that reputedly had the first electric lights in Dorchester. The building would later have three additional stories added to it and be known jointly as the "Upham Building" and "Odd Fellow's Building."

By 1900, Upham's Corner was a thriving shopping district, with the Upham Building having been constructed in 1884 to replace the earlier building. Pictured are "The Dorchester," an apartment building (left), Winthrop Hall, the Upham Building, and the S.B. Pierce Building (right).

The S.B. Pierce Building was built by J. Homer Pierce, on the site of his father's former home. Built at the junction of Columbia Road and Ramsey Street, it was Dorchester's own "Flat Iron" building, with Cefrino's Market on the first floor and offices above. Its arched windows and massive cornice made for an impressive approach to Upham's Corner. On the left is the Upham Building, and on the right is the Baker Memorial Church.

Columbia Road was known as "Boston Street," the road leading to Boston for two centuries. However, by the 1890s, it was graded and laid out as connecting Franklin Park to Castle Island. Its green space and trees made an impressive drive for the new "horseless carriages."

COLUMBIA ROAD.

Many are the years that have rolled around
Since near this spot, on sacred ground,
A band of Pilgrims there did meet,
Laid out a road, called Boston street.

The old Town Meeting was then begun,
Schools were started, free to every one;
The next best thing they thought about,
Was building roads o'er the best route.

The "Mary and John" brought Wolcott and Clapp,
Stoughton and Minot, with muscle and snap;
They were the men, with others as good,
They built Boston road, and well it has stood.

To finish this road, built crooked and wrong,
We are gathered to-day, a joyful throng;
To hail and to greet the long waited for day,
Meeting to widen our Boulevard way.

To Quincy and Folsom hearty thanks are due,
Lott and McCormick get thanks from you;
A citizen host helped the scheme along,
Faithfully they worked, pushing good and strong.

Now, for "**Columbia Road**" three cheers we'll give,
Long may it stand, long may it live;
And in coming years, an anthem will rise,
Calling us blessed, and very wise.

Dorchester, September 9, 1897.

61

The Dorchester Municipal Building was built at the corner of Columbia Road and Bird Street. With a branch library, gymnasiums, and office space, it was built just west of Upham's Corner and still serves a vitally important need in the community.

The Strand Theatre was Dorchester's "Multi-Million Dollar Palace" and was opened on Armistice Day, November 11, 1918. Built on the former Dyer Estate, it faced Columbia Road and offered mirrored foyers, crystal chandeliers, fountains with goldfish, and an organ to accompany the silent movies. During intermission, patrons could dance to a twenty-one piece orchestra or marvel at the marble and bronze interiors.

Samuel Downer was a merchant who dealt in whale oil. Through experimentation with the distillation of oil, he invented kerosene and changed how America lit the dark. His estate was at the corner of Pleasant Street and Downer Avenue, and here he hybridized the "Downer Late" cherry.

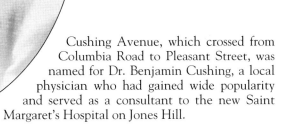

Cushing Avenue, which crossed from Columbia Road to Pleasant Street, was named for Dr. Benjamin Cushing, a local physician who had gained wide popularity and served as a consultant to the new Saint Margaret's Hospital on Jones Hill.

The Baker Memorial Church was built at the corner of Columbia Road and Cushing Avenue, through the bequest of Miss Sarah Baker, a band box maker. A devout Methodist, Miss Baker made wood band boxes that were covered in colorful wallpaper. If a woman of that period was particularly well dressed, it was popularly said that she "looked as if she just stepped out of a band box." Miss Baker's bequest was invested and the church built.

Saint Paul's Church was built by Maginnis and Walsh, on Hartford Street, beside the Hooper family's estate "Oakland." Completed in 1937, this impressive church, with its massive, turreted tower, rose from a hill to overlook most of Dorchester.

Saint Mary's Infant Asylum was for the children of parents who had not sought the benefit of clergy. These children, seen here enjoying the sun-filled eastern lawn of the former Greene Estate, were looked after by the Sisters of Charity.

Saint Margaret's Hospital became one of New England's foremost gynecological hospitals, with one out of every two births in Boston taking place here during the 1940s and 1950s. From left to right are Helen Kennedy, Ann Hannigan, and Eileen Mitchell. They were members of the last graduating class of Saint Margaret's School of Nursing in 1951.

The Upham family grave at the Old North Burying Ground was marked by a simple white marble headstone. Seen here, students of the Edward Everett School plant daffodils to mark one site of the "neighborhood history" course offered by Historic Education.

A student at the Edward Everett School helps plant daffodils on the graves of three slaves who had belonged to the Oliver and Foster families of Dorchester. "Betty," "Cambridge," and "Ann" must have been devoted and adored servants as these slate headstones commemorate their lives whereas the graves of most slaves went unmarked.

Six
Field's Corner and Commercial Point

The Robinson House was on Adams Street between Arcadia and Robinson Streets. Built in 1788 by John Robinson, the house was demolished in 1917 to make way for the New England Telephone Building.

William Taylor Adams' house was on Dorchester Avenue, at the corner of Faulkner Street. This house was designed by Luther Briggs Jr., an architect and land surveyor, and stood where the ramps to the Fields Corner T are now located.

William Taylor Adams' *nom de plume* was "Oliver Optic." His "Boat Builder" series of books was popular reading material for nineteenth-century boys. An educator-turned-writer, he wrote uplifting educational books with a moral story.

The Whitten House was on Centre Street, between Dorchester Avenue and Adams Street. Built by Boston City Alderman Charles V. Whitten, it boasted a fabled rose garden and a piazza that wrapped itself around all four sides of the house.

Blanche Street had two impressive houses designed by architect John A. Fox. On the left is D.J. Cutter's own house, at 15 Blanche Street, which has unusually fine details, a modified hipped roof, and impressive chimneys.

O'Keefe's Grocery Store was opened at the corner of Dorchester Avenue and Charles Street. Providing tea, coffee, and a general supply of groceries, O'Keefe's would later be merged into what became First National Markets.

NOTICE.

ISAAC FIELD, GROCERIES.

The Citizens of Dor-
chester are hereby respectfully informed that by calling at the

OLD STAND GROCERY STORE,

HARRISON SQUARE,

they can find a general assortment of Groceries, consisting in part of
BEST FAMILY FLOUR, CHOICE TEAS, SUGAR, OIL, &C.
DAIRY BUTTER AND FRUIT OF ALL KINDS,
and a complete assortment of FANCY GROCERIES.
Also, Crockery, Glass, Stone and Earthen Ware,
all of which will be offered at low prices for cash, the motto being *large sales and small profits.* The Subscriber tenders his acknowledgments to his customers for their liberal patronage in times past, and respectfully solicits a continuance of the same, assuring them that no pains shall be spared on his part to give them the freshest goods the market affords, as he is daily replenishing his stock. Goods delivered to any part of the town, free of expense.
N. B. Fishing and Pic-Nic Parties, supplied as usual.

ISAAC FIELD.

Harrison Square, Dorchester, April 1st, 1852.

Isaac Field's grocery store, at the junction of Adams Street and Dorchester Avenue, supplied "a general assortment of groceries" for local residents. Originally known as "Dalrymple Junction," the intersection was renamed Field's Corner in honor of Isaac and Enos Field, brothers who had one store in the area and another at Harrison Square.

The Municipal Building, at the corner of Adams and Arcadia Streets, was designed by Boston City Architect George Clough. When completed in the 1870s, it had Dorchester's only court room, police station, and library! Today, it has been restored by the Fields Corner CDC, and has been adapted for numerous businesses.

Police Station 11 shared space at the Field's Corner Municipal Building. The Dorchester Police force poses on the steps for this group portrait at the turn of the century.

Sturtevant Street was laid out with mills and workers' housing near Field's Corner. Named for Benjamin Sturtevant, owner of the Blowing mills at Clayton and Park Streets, it is depicted with both residential and commercial aspects.

Clayton Street was a mud-filled street during the spring, when horse and carriages brought supplies to the mills. In the center of the photograph is the Sturtevant Mill, which produced blowers for furnaces and mills.

Park Street divided the Town Field (left) from the holding yards of the street trolleys on the right. Town Field was left to Dorchester by Christopher Gibson, an early settler, and was known as "Gibson Field." Later, the clubhouse was built and the area on the right was developed in the 1960s as a shopping mall.

The Casey Club was founded for young men by Representative Dick Casey, as somewhere they could be supervised and receive direction. Casey, a Red Sox fan and ardent supporter of the youth of Dorchester, was elated when the Casey Club Baseball Team became the Boston Park League's Champions in 1940. The Town Field at Field's Corner was named "Casey Field" in his memory.

The baseball club of the "Casey Club" is pictured here with their mentor Dick Casey, at Casey Field in Dorchester.

The football club of the "Casey Club" is photographed here seated in the bleachers of Town Field with Dick Casey on the far left. Notice the waterboys in the foreground with water buckets marked "Casey Club."

Harrison Square, named in 1841 for President William Henry Harrison, was laid out by the surveyor Luther Briggs Jr. With the Old Colony Railroad line nearby connecting Boston to the South Shore, new residents had large houses built along Mill Street.

Mill Street at Blanche Street is seen here in the mid-nineteenth century while a coal sloop unloads at the wharf of D.J. Cutter & Company. The newly-laid out streets and the gas street lamps offer a glimpse into how rural Dorchester actually was in the 1860s.

This area of Harrison Square included Blanche Street, which was on the eastern edge of the new neighborhood. The building on the right is now the site of Linda Mae's Bakery and Restaurant, and the view seen here between the houses is of Savin Hill.

Commercial Point, seen here from Pope's Hill, shows Neponset Avenue in the foreground, with the Farrington and Hunnewell Silversmiths on the left at the corner of Tilesboro Street. This interesting view shows how open the land east of Pope's Hill was in the nineteenth century.

The bathing beach along Tenean Beach was a stretch of fine sand that had bathing houses and boards used for diving. Today, this area has been reconstructed, with Morrissey Boulevard crossing at this beach and Tenean Beach having moved to the west.

Numerous coal scuttles are docked at Commercial Point with the new gas tanks rising in the background. For many years, the tanks rose and fell with the quantity of man-made gas they contained.

Barque Warwick Cove was a small creek that flooded at high tide. The area was named for the barque *Warwick*, a British ship that went aground in the seventeenth century; for many years, the hull could be seen where it went aground. Today this area is Victory Road and the cove has been filled in for the Armory.

The twin mansions of Newell and Niles, China Trade merchants, were built on Commercial Point in the early nineteenth century. These houses were for partners who traded with the South Sea Island of Tinian, bringing gums, spices, and luxury items to Dorchester, where they sold their goods.

Commercial Point, looking towards Harrison Square, was a once thriving neighborhood of small farms, mills, and wharves; the area also had extensive whaling concerns in the 1830s and 1840s.

The Bradley House, a substantial Federal house with views of Dorchester Bay, was located on Commercial Street at Commercial Point. The entire Bradley family, including the family horse, turned out for this photograph.

Another view of Commercial Street, at Commercial Point, shows the extent of the demolition. By 1888, the former neighborhood was obliterated.

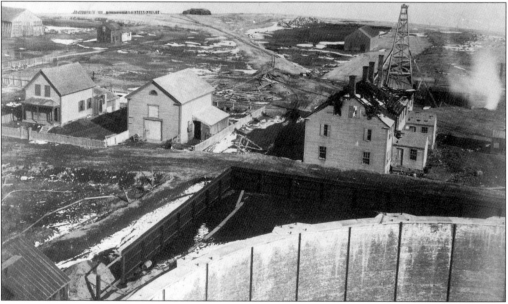

Seen here from a hot air balloon, Commercial Point has been abandoned and the construction of the tanks for gas production are being laid. In the rear, Commercial Street's houses and barns await demolition. Today, none of these structures, other than the one gas tank, remain located at Commercial Point.

The buildings of Commercial Point were systematically levelled in the 1880s to ensure safety in the production of gas by the Boston Gas Works. This is a view of Dorchester Bay and the Harbor, with Thompson Island on the right.

One company on Commercial Point was D.J. Cutter & Company, a coal and firewood dealer. The horse-drawn wagon (left) delivered heating supplies throughout Dorchester, and the youngsters to the right may be the next generation of Cutters, since the company still exists as one of Dorchester's oldest suppliers of heating fuel.

The Capen House was at the corner of Washington and Dunlap Streets. According to local lore, it was built by Barnard Capen. In 1919 it was moved to Milton, Massachusetts, as the summerhouse of Professor Webster of Harvard.

The Davenport House was at the corner of Washington Street and Wheatland Avenue. Built in the late eighteenth century, this farmhouse, with its impressive stone wall, would survive until 1910.

Seven
Codman Square

Seen here from Norfolk Street, the Second Church's spire was visible from all approaches. On the right are the Codman Square Branch, the Boston Public Library (now the Codman Square Health Center), and various commercial structures.

The Second Church was built in 1805 and dedicated in 1808, as Dorchester's population increase had precluded a new meeting house. However, Reverend John Codman adhered to the traditional Congregational belief, while the First Parish Church adopted Unitarianism. A fierce rivalry developed and was not healed for decades. The clock was given by Walter Baker, a parishioner, whose chocolate mill was at Lower Mills.

The Codman Mansion was on Codman Hill, just west of Reverend John Codman's church. Built by the Thayers, it was purchased by the Codman family and stood at the junction of Washington and Ogden Streets and Wilmington Avenue. After Codman's death in 1847, the family later rented the house to a female academy known as Miss Dodge's. Students are shown here at the estate's gate.

The Christopher Gibson School was built on School Street and named for an early settler of Dorchester who had left a bequest to the town to benefit the schools. Designed by Boston architect Gridley J. Fox Bryant, this Italianate school was in marked contrast to the one-room schoolhouse of a generation earlier.

The Dorchester Town Hall (right) was built in 1816 at the corner of Washington and Norfolk Streets. After the religious controversy between the First and Second Churches, the separation of church and state became complete with the building of this hall. To the left is Baker's General Store, which was operated by Dr. James Baker, founder of the chocolate mill. It was known as Baker's Corner until 1848, when it was renamed "Codman Square" in memory of Reverend John Codman.

Dorchester's town government was established in 1636, at a town meeting. For over two centuries, this form of government met to direct the town's affairs. Seen in this photograph, taken in 1869, are the last selectmen of Dorchester. From left to right are William Pope, James Humphreys Upham (chairman), James Swan, and Thomas Temple. On January 4, 1870, Dorchester was officially annexed to the City of Boston.

86

The Gleason Factory (left), with workers' housing, was located on Washington Street, opposite School Street. Gleason was successful in business, but when the factory burned in 1871, Gleason retired rather than start over. The site of the factory became "Mother's Rest," a park overlooking Dorchester Bay.

Roswell Gleason was a britanniaware manufacturer located near Four Corners. From 1822 on, he produced a new form of pewter known as "britannia," creating beakers, bowls, candlesticks, oil lamps, and tea and coffee pots. By 1850 he was silverplating base metal, and is considered the first person to have used this new process in the United States.

"Lilacs" was Gleason's house, located at the corner of Washington and Park Streets. Built in 1837, it was testimony to Gleason's success. With a circular carriage drive, playing fountains, and garden statuary, it encompassed over 40 acres. Following a fire in the early part of this century, the house was turned around to face Claybourne Street. The house was destroyed by arson in 1979.

The Robert Ball Hughes House stands at the corner of Washington and School Streets. Built by the Spaulding family, the house was later the home of Ball Hughes, a noted sculptor and artist.

The Torrey House was built at the corner of Washington Street and Melville Avenue. Designed by the Boston firm of Cabot & Chandler, it survived until the 1930s, when it was demolished and replaced by a gas station.

The Terhune House is a stately Colonial Revival mansion built on Melville Avenue by a Boston shoe and boot manufacturer. Seen in his carriage outside his house is a typical "street car suburb" resident of Dorchester.

Dorchester High School was built at the corner of Talbot Avenue and Centre Street. Designed by Hartwell, Richardson, and Driver and built in 1895, it was later to become Dorchester High School for Girls when a new school was built for boys on Dunbar Avenue in 1928. In the 1950s, it became Girls' Latin School, later Boston Latin Academy, and today has been adapted as Latin Academy Apartments.

The Codman Square Branch, Boston Public Library, was built on the site of the former Town Hall. Designed as a Colonial Revival library, with a cupola and Chinese Chippendale roof balustrade, the interior was of golden oak with floors that squeaked with every step. Today, it has been adapted as the Codman Square Health Center.

The Dorchester Womens Club was built on Centre Street, beside the Second Church. With Ripley Hall (left) and Whiton Hall, the six hundred-member club hosted lectures, dances, and musicals in order to raise money for worthy causes. During the 1940s and thereafter, many Dorchester brides were to hold their wedding receptions in this elegant clubhouse.

A. Warren Gould was a local architect who lived on Waldeck Street. Many of his residential designs were on Waldeck, Lyndsey, and Larchmont Streets and Melville Avenue. His design of the Dorchester Womens Club shows how adept he was at the style of the Colonial Revival.

The Lucy Stone House was on Boutwell Street. This was the home of Lucy Stone—the first woman to graduate from college (Oberlin College), the first woman to maintain her maiden name after her marriage, and the first woman editor (of *The Womans Journal*). Lucy Stone was an anti-slavery advocate, as was her husband Henry Browne Blackwell. They lived on Pope's Hill.

Eight
Pope's Hill and Cedar Grove

The Ward-McCondry-King House was a Federal mansion, built on Adams Street, opposite Lonsdale and Mallet Streets. The second owner was Captain McCondry, who was involved in the China Trade and erected a tea house in the shape of a pagoda on "Ginger Hill," now known as Daly Street.

The Thomas Pierce House was on Adams Street, just north of Minot Street. The small house was next to the cinema at Adams Village and was later demolished. The Shell Gas Station is on its former site.

Seen here from Mill Street in 1880, Pope's Hill rises from Neponset Avenue. Numerous houses were being built in the neighborhood at that time, and the orchard in the foreground was for sale for development.

The Pierce House on Oakton Avenue, just east of Adams Street. Built by Robert and Ann Pierce, *c.* 1650, it has been preserved by the Society for the Preservation of New England Antiquities.

The Lewis House stands at the corner of Adams and Wrentham Streets. This large Italianate house had extensive grounds with greenhouses, and was the home of local architect Edwin J. Lewis Jr. Ironically, although Lewis designed and built hundreds of houses, he never lived in a house of his own design.

The Ward-McCondry-King House was a three-story Federal mansion that was the home of three families in less than one hundred years. The Kings were a Boston family who moved to Dorchester in the 1860s and for whom "King Square" (the junction of Neponset Avenue, Adams, and Parkman Streets) was named.

The Laban Pratt House was on Pope's Hill, at the corner of what is now Laban Pratt Road. A lumber dealer at Port Norfolk, Pratt was a successful business man who had local architect John A. Fox design his house.

The Dorchester Mutual Fire Insurance Company was built on Walnut Street at Port Norfolk. The building was also used as the post office and apothecary shop and was designed by Charles Austin Wood.

Charles Austin Wood was an architect who lived at Port Norfolk in Dorchester.

The auditorium of the Mary Hemenway School was on the third floor, with massive arched windows. In the photograph, the flowers and vegetables grown by the students in their "Victory Garden" are arranged for display beneath a life-sized statue of Athena Nike.

A cairn was erected in the "Victory Garden," on the former Ward-McCondry-King Estate by the students of the Mary Hemenway School. The school, in the rear, was at the corner of Adams and King Streets. The students planted gardens during World War I.

Seen here from Commercial Point, Pope's Hill was a tree-covered hill that had been named for the Pope family, lumber merchants in Dorchester and Machias, Maine. Notice the ship weathervane on the cupola to the left.

Avis Haynes (left) and Ruth Raycraft pose on the hill opposite the Raycraft Farm on Minot Street. The land would later be developed, with Charlemont Street being laid out after World War I.

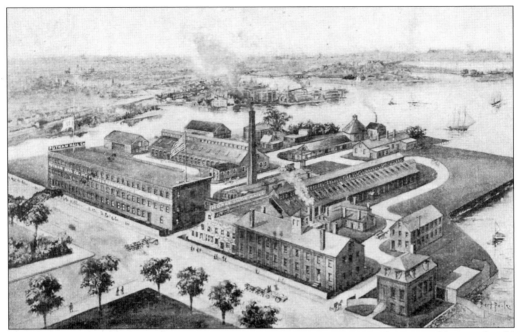

The Putnam Nail Company was founded by S.S. Putnam as a manufacturer of hot and cold forged nails. Located on Port Norfolk, Putnam produced horse-shoe nails that were among the best-produced nails in the United States in the nineteenth century.

Edwin J. Lewis Jr. was a local architect who had graduated from MIT and served an apprenticeship with the Boston architectural firm of Peabody and Stearns. From 1887 until his death in 1937, he pursued an independent career designing residences, commercial buildings, and over forty Unitarian churches in the United States and Canada.

S.S. Pierce's birthplace was later converted into his summerhouse. A rambling series of additions, it stood on what is now Gallivan Boulevard, the site of Saint Brendan's Church. Pierce's daughter, "Miss Etta," lived here in the summer until her death in 1920, after which her heirs sold the estate for subdivision. Notice the three-deckers on Minot Street on the right.

S.S. Pierce was a purveyor of fancy groceries to generations of Bostonians. Born Samuel Stillman Pierce, the son of Daniel and Lydia Pierce, he rose to become one of New England's most successful businessmen.

Lucy Stone is one of Dorchester's best-known achievers. Born in West Brookfield, Massachusetts, she worked her way through Oberlin College and lectured on the evils of slavery. After her marriage to Henry Browne Blackwell, she insisted on maintaining her maiden name, became the first female editor (*The Womans Journal*), and upon her death she was the first person in the United States to be cremated.

Alice Stone Blackwell was the only child of Lucy Stone and Henry Browne Blackwell. After her mother's death in 1893, Miss Blackwell assumed the editorship of *The Womans Journal*. She leased the Pope's Hill house for a dollar to an inner-city settlement house so that "children might breathe clean air and enjoy a day in the country."

In 1917, the first graduating class at Saint Anne's Church posed for this class portrait on the church lawn.

Saint Anne's Band, posing on the lawn at the church, was one of New England's premier marching bands. With distinctive uniforms and an assured air, they won numerous competitions.

Saint Brenden's Church was established as a parish in 1929, with the first masses being said in a garage at the corner of Gallivan Boulevard and Granite Avenue.

The interior of the garage was transformed on Saturday evenings when drapes were hung over the windows, an alter erected, and chairs set up for Sunday masses. Saint Brendan's parishioners used the garage for five years until a church was built at the corner of Gallivan Boulevard and Saint Brendan Road.

Gallivan Boulevard was named for Representative James Gallivan of the United States House of Representatives. Once known as Marsh and Codman Streets, it was joined in 1928 and renamed in memory of Gallivan.

The Dorchester Methodist Episcopal Church was founded in 1816, and this church was built in 1829 on Washington Street, next to the Edmund J. Baker House.

The trolley that connects Ashmont Station to Mattapan Square entitles Dorchester to be included in *Ripley's Believe It or Not*. The trolley runs through a cemetary (Cedar Grove), supposedly the only such claim in this country!

In 1875, the Dorchester Methodist Episcopal Church built a new church, with a soaring spire that could be seen for miles. On the left can be seen a duplex house, built for the many workers in the industrial concerns along the Neponset River.

Nine
Lower Mills

The Dorchester School of Music (left) and the Bispham Block (designed by Joseph T. Greene) were at the corner of Washington and Adams Street near the bridge spanning the Neponset River. The Pierce Mill of Baker's Chocolate Company is on the far left.

The Milton Village Inn was at the corner of what is now Washington Street and Dorchester Avenue. Built in 1793, it was an inn where travelers could obtain a hot meal or a bed for the night. Today it is the site of Dark Horse Antiques, an antique shop of "collectibles and oddities."

Dr. James Baker had been a storekeeper at Baker's Corner (now Codman Square) before he met John Hannon, a penniless Irish immigrant who had the skill of making chocolate. With Hannon, Baker financed a mill in the Lower Mills and chocolate was produced as early as 1765.

The Pierce Mill was built in 1872 as part of the expansion plans of Henry L. Pierce. Designed by Bradlee and Winslow, the mill was named for Pierce who was mayor of Boston at the time of its erection.

Henry Lillie Pierce was a step-nephew of Walter Baker, and two years after his uncle's death he was allowed to lease the chocolate mill at the Lower Mills. From 1854 until 1884, he produced chocolate under the name "Walter Baker & Company," paying to the trustees of the Baker Estate a substantial sum for this privilege. Pierce served as mayor of Boston in 1872 and 1877.

The Webb Mill was built in 1882, at the corner of Adams and Eliot Streets on the Milton side of the Neponset River. Named for Webb Chocolate Company, it was one of three former competitors of Baker's to be purchased and incorporated into Walter Baker and Company. Preston's, Webb's (formerly Webb and Twombley), and Ware's Chocolate Companies all produced chocolate in the Lower Mills in the mid-nineteenth century, so that the Lower Mills earned the appellation "Chocolate Village."

The Dorchester Lower Mills included the Forbes Mill (left), the Administration Building (center), and the Pierce Mill (right). The early nineteenth-century granite bridge is seen spanning the Neponset River below a more modern bridge.

Edmund James Baker was the grandson of Dr. James Baker and half-brother of Walter Baker. A surveyor by trade, he drew maps of Dorchester and Milton and was postmaster of Milton at one time.

Edmund James Baker demolished his father's house in 1872, and had a large mansion built at the corner of Washington and Richmond Streets. On the far left is the Safford House, where Lincoln stayed in 1847, and the spire of the Methodist Episcopal church can be seen rising above the roof.

Richmond Hall, named for the Reverend Joseph Richmond, was originally the Third Religious Society in Dorchester. After a larger church was built in 1840, this was converted into a hall, and here Abraham Lincoln spoke to Dorchester residents in 1847 when he toured New England on behalf of Zachary Taylor. Today the hall is now an apartment building and stands beside the Greene House.

Joseph Greene, a local architect, lived with his family in this house on Washington Street opposite Richmond Street. Greene designed the Lithgow Building at Codman Square, the now-lost Bispham Block at Lower Mills, and numerous houses on Adams, Carruth, and Beaumont Streets in Dorchester.

The Village Congregational Church was at the corner of River and Old Morton Streets, just a couple of blocks west of Washington Street. This simple church was later enlarged, but after World War II it disbanded and joined the Milton Congregational Church.

Cedar Grove Cemetery was laid out by Luther Briggs Jr. in the 1860s as an arboretum cemetery. On the banks of the Neponset River, Cedar Grove was originally known as "Gin Plain," as junipers in the area produced berries that could be used in the distillation of gin. The fountain, stately trees, and well-kept grounds still offer a place for nature walks.

This Hibbard painting shows Vermont in Winter. With a mottled effect, more precise than impressionism, Aldro T. Hibbard had a successful career as an artist.

Aldro T. Hibbard was a popular painter whose winter scenes evoked New England's past. Born in the Lower Mills, and a member of the baseball team at Dorchester High School, he is one of the many artists Dorchester can claim, among them Childe Hassam, Edmund Tarbell, Robert Ball Hughes, and William T. Carleton.

Ten
Peabody Square

Jacques Market was built in 1884, as marked by stones in the gable, at the corner of Dorchester Avenue and Ashmont Street. Peabody Square, named after Colonel Oliver White Peabody, who was founder of Kidder, Peabody, & Company, was the location of the Old Colony Railroad at Ashmont (far right).

Peabody Square is the intersection of Dorchester Avenue and Ashmont Street. All Saints Episcopal Church (left) was designed by Cram, Wentworth, and Goodhue, and completed in 1893. The Peabody (right) was designed by Edwin J. Lewis Jr. as professional offices on the first floor and apartments above. The square was a small lot of land with a drinking fountain and a clock designed by William Downer Austin.

Nathan Carruth was the first president of the Old Colony Railroad, which connected Boston to the South Shore. His estate was known as "Beechmont" and was bounded by Carruth, Beaumont, Ashmont, and Adams Streets.

The Herbert Shaw Carruth House was built on Beaumont Street, the former carriage drive to his father's estate. Nathan Carruth had purchased a large tract of land in Dorchester in 1847, and the estate was developed after his death.

Herbert Shaw Carruth was the son of Nathan Carruth, and after his father's death he began the subdivision of the estate for residences. Beaumont Street, a carriage drive to his father's house, became built up with large houses designed by local architects Edwin J. Lewis Jr., John A. Fox, Joseph Greene, and A. Warren Gould.

The Welles House stood at the corner of Washington Street and Welles Avenue and had such illustrious tenants at General Henry Knox, Daniel Webster, Madam Cobb (a daughter of Reverend John Codman), and the Welles family, for whom the town of Wellesley, Massachusetts, was named. The house was demolished in 1893 for the Pierce School.

Harrison H. Atwood was a local architect who lived on Alban Street on Ashmont Hill. He designed the Emily Fifield School on Dundar Avenue and the now-demolished Henry Lillie Pierce School that stood at the corner of Washington Street and Welles Avenue.

Mayor John Fitzgerald lived in a large Victorian mansion at the corner of Welles Avenue and Harley Street. His daughter Rose married Joseph Kennedy, later ambassador to the Court of Saint James, and they were the parents of the late President John Fitzgerald Kennedy.

Thomas A. Hibbard served as mayor of Boston between the terms of his neighbor John F. Fitzgerald. His house was at the corner of Beaumont and Fairfax Streets and was designed by the architect John A. Fox.

The Emmons House on Harley Street was built by the founders of the Stanley Steamer Automobile for their sister, Chansonetta Stanley Emmons. A large, turreted Queen Anne house, it still stands on Ashmont Hill.

Edmund Tarbell was an important Impressionistic artist who lived on Alban Street. His paintings depicted family scenes, gardens, and pastoral landscapes favored by Impressionists.

Charles Belledeau is seen in his carriage in front of his house at the corner of Roslin and Ocean Streets. This Victorian house was modernized when a Colonial Revival porch, Palladian window, and a swell bay front entrance with leaded-glass windows were added.

One member of the Dorchester Gentlemen's Driving Club was Mayor John Fitzgerald (center), seen here receiving a sterling loving cup for his win. Known for his rendition of "Sweet Adeline," he would sing this popular tune as women, reputedly, swooned.

Franklin Field was a large park at the corner of Blue Hill and Talbot Avenue. The Dorchester Gentlemen's Driving Club raced their horses in a sulky at the track. Seen here at the start, a driver awaits the signal.

During the winter, sledding on specially iced runs made for swift enjoyment at Franklin Park.

Eleven
Franklin Park and Franklin Field

The entrance to the Franklin Park Zoo was a monumental gateway with eight columns that were originally in the rotunda of the Customs House and were removed when the tower was built by Peabody and Stearns. The approach and entrance were impressive designs that enhanced the greenspace.

The bears included not only polar bears, but grizzly bears, black bears, and brown bears, all of which were in large cages that might resemble their den.

The Bird Cage was a marvel of soaring stone arches with waterways that allowed swans, ducks, and pelicans to entertain the visitors to the zoo while smaller birds flew above.

The Elephant House was a large concrete building where African and Indian elephants were stabled.

Franklin Park was laid out by Frederick Law Olmstead as the jewel in the Emerald Necklace, greenspace that surrounded Boston. The vast acreage—once composed of seven farms—included tennis courts, badminton courts, open spaces, and a golf course.

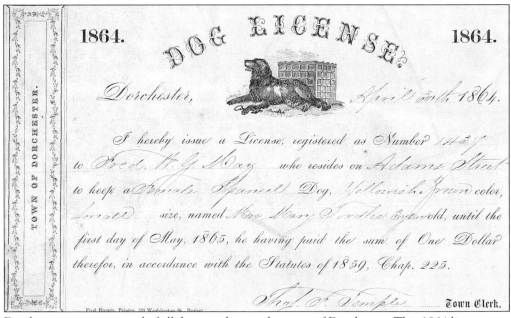

DORCHESTER ATHENEUM.

Incorporated A. D. 1857.

No. *141.* | *One* Shares. | $ *20*

Be it Known, That *George Newhall* of *Dorchester* State of *Massachusetts* is entitled to *One* Shares in the Capital Stock of the *Dorchester Atheneum,* transferable only at the rooms of said Corporation by the said *Geo. Newhall* personally, or by Attorney, and on surrendering this Certificate.

In Testimony Whereof, The President and Treasurer have signed this Certificate at Dorchester, the *Eighth* day of *January* A. D. *1859.*

John G Nano President.

A. White Treasurer.

T. Groom & Co., Stationers.

The Dorchester Athenaeum was a private library located on the corner of Pond and East Cottage Streets. One purchased shares of stock to become a member and in order to be allowed to use the collection. After Dorchester was annexed to the City of Boston, the need for a private library ceased, and a branch library of the Boston Public Library was opened at Field's Corner.

DOG LICENSE.

1864.   **1864.**

TOWN OF DORCHESTER.

Dorchester,   *April 30th 1864.*

I hereby issue a License, registered as Number *1457* to *Fred. W. G. May* who resides on *Adams Street* to keep a *Female Spaniel Dog, Yellowish Brown* color, *Small* size, named *Mrs. Mary Fowdler* years old, until the first day of May, 1865, he having paid the sum of *One Dollar* therefor, in accordance with the Statutes of 1859, Chap. 225.

Thos. F. Temple Town Clerk.

Fred. Rogers, Printer, 179 Washington St., Boston.

Dog licenses were required of all dogs residing in the town of Dorchester. This 1864 license was for a canine pet of the May family of Adams Street on Meeting House Hill.

The Dorchester Express Company, owned by the Mitchell family, would have stevedores deliver, or return, trunks from Dorchester homes to ships sailing for Europe. Seen here, two employees pose for the camera, but the horse does not look happy to be pulling a load of steamer trunks!

The annual Dorchester Day Parade is celebrated on the first Sunday in June, when marching bands, floats, and local politicians walk the length of Dorchester Avenue..

Acknowledgments

When Raymond L. Flynn, former mayor of Boston and now ambassador to the Vatican, named me the Dorchester Town Historian, I felt that many aspects of Dorchester's local history had already been recorded in my articles in the *Dorchester Community News*. However, this book, published by Arcadia, is issued in the twenty-fifth year since I first became fascinated by Dorchester's history.

I would also like to thank the following individuals for their continued support and encouragement: Daniel Ahlin, Leah Clapp Allen, Robin Alsop, Joan Banfield, Anthony Bognanno, Paul and Helen Buchanan, Sean Cahill, Mary Jo Campbell (Lower Mills Branch, Boston Public Library), Elizabeth Clapp, Clara Clapp, Reverend Mary Clapp, Edith Clifford, Regina Clifton, Mary G. Connell, Lorna Condon (Society for the Preservation of New England Antiquities), Reverend Elizabeth Curtiss (the First Parish Church in Dorchester), Marion Diener, Rupert Davis, Lydia Bowman Edwards, John B. Fox, the late Walter S. Fox, Catherine Flannery, Ardelle Moseley Fullerton, Edward W. Gordon, Philip Gavin, Joseph Gildea, Jean Goldman, Roger Greene, Virginia Holbrook, Gertrude Hooper, Elizabeth Bradford Hough, James Z. Kyprianos, William Laughran, Fred Lyons, Margaret Lamb, John F. May, Evelyn Menconi, Dagmar Pierce Merna, Reverend Michael Parise, William H. Pear, Mark Pickering, Daniel Pierce, Roger S. Pierce, Sally Pierce (the Boston Athenaeum), the late Ruth Raycraft, Dennis Ryan, Anthony and Mary Mitchell Sammarco, Rosemary Sammarco, Sylvia Sandeen, Robert Bayard Severy, Helen Ruggles Shaw, Letitia Carruth Stone, William V. Tripp, William Varrell, Virginia M. White, and Marion Woodbridge.

All royalties from this book will be directed to The Sammarco Fund of the Lower Mills Branch, Boston Public Library.